SAINTS FOR GIRLS

How to use this Sticker Book

Read the names of the Saints in the book,
and choose the Saint that fits in the appropriate space.

You can use the stickers more than once.

You can also use these stickers to make holy cards
and greeting cards or to decorate your own books.

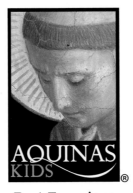

Bart Tesoriero
Illustrated by Michael Adams

ISBN 1-936020-47-8
Copyright © 2010, 2012 Aquinas Kids, Phoenix, Arizona.
First Edition, 2010; Second Edition, 2012
Fifth Printing, July, 2017

Mothers and Servants

Mary Queen of All Saints

Patroness of All Saints and Angels

Feast Day: August 22

God gave Jesus to us through Mary, and Jesus gave Mary to us through John, His beloved apostle, at the foot of the Cross. She alone is full of grace, and we draw from her abundance. Mary is the Queen of all saints because she cooperated most faithfully with all the rich graces God granted her. Because of her fullness of grace and splendor of virtues, Mary is raised above all saints as Queen. ***Dear Mary, Queen of All Saints, pray for us!***

Saint Anne

Patroness of Grandmothers

Feast Day: July 26

Saint Anne, the spouse of Saint Joachim, was chosen by God to be the mother of Mary, His own blessed Mother on earth. Tradition holds that Anne bore Mary in her old age, and then consecrated her to the Lord. From then on she watched and prayed, until God called her to heaven with Himself. Many Christians throughout the world since the very early days of the Church have loved and honored Saint Anne, the grandmother of Jesus! ***Saint Anne, pray for us!***

Saint Martha

Patroness of Homemakers

Feast Day: July 29

Martha, the sister of Mary and Lazarus, loved to cook and care for Jesus, a frequent guest at her home. Observing that Martha was often worried and distracted, Jesus reminded her that only one thing was truly important—listening to Him. Martha learned her lesson, and later on, when Lazarus died, Martha trusted Jesus to raise him from the dead. She is recognized today as the patroness of all who serve others with love.
Saint Martha, pray for us!

Saint Veronica

Patroness of Photographers

Feast Day: July 12

According to tradition, Saint Veronica is the woman of Jerusalem who wiped the face of Jesus with her veil on His way to Calvary. The cloth was imprinted with the image of Christ's face. Her name is probably derived from 'vera icon', meaning 'true image'. The relic is still preserved in Saint Peter's Basilica, and the memory of Veronica's act of charity is commemorated in the Stations of the Cross. ***Saint Veronica, pray for us!***

Brides of Christ and Martyrs

Saint Lucy

Patroness of Eyesight

Feast Day: December 13

Saint Lucy is a greatly beloved third century Italian martyr. A young man to whom Lucy had been promised in marriage accused her as a Christian, and the Roman governor had her eyes gouged out. God miraculously restored Lucy's eyesight, and the governor reacted by setting her on fire. Again, God saved her. Finally, Lucy was martyred with a dagger.

Saint Lucy, pray for us!

Saint Cecilia

Patroness of Musicians and Singers

Feast Day: November 22

Cecilia, a beautiful and noble Roman maiden, had vowed her virginity to God. Her parents had her married to Valerian, who was baptized and gave himself to God after hearing heavenly music on their wedding night. The Romans killed Valerian and commanded Cecilia to be burned in a furnace. But the flames had no power over her body, and so the executioner beheaded her. In 177 the virgin Saint Cecilia gave back her pure spirit to Christ.

Saint Cecilia, pray for us!

Saint Apollonia

Patroness of Those with Dental Ailments

Feast Day: February 9

Saint Apollonia was born in third century Egypt and spent her entire life preaching the word of God. In 249, pagan persecutors arrested Apollonia, who courageously declared, "I am a Christian and I love and serve the true God." Her persecutors angrily resorted to torture. She stood firm and refused to give up even when they smashed her teeth and then knocked them out of her mouth. The pagans told her that if she did not deny Jesus, she would be thrown into a raging fire. Rather than deny her faith in Jesus, she jumped into the burning fire herself. When the pagans saw Apollonia's heroic faith, many of them were converted and accepted Christ.

Saint Apollonia, pray for us!

Preachers and Princesses

Saint Barbara

Patroness of Builders and Protection from Storms

Feast Day: December 4

Saint Barbara's pagan father hid her in a lonely tower. Even so, a priest converted and baptized Barbara, which greatly angered her father. He denounced her before the civil tribunal who ordered her to be tortured. Barbara held on to her faith in Jesus, and in a rage, her father drew his sword and beheaded her himself. On his way home he was struck and killed by a flash of lightning. Saint Barbara is honored as the patroness of architects, because of her imprisonment in the tower, and she is also often invoked during thunderstorms and lightning.

Saint Barbara, pray for us!

Saint Catherine of Alexandria

Patroness of Philosophers and Preachers

Feast Day: November 25

Saint Catherine was a noble Catholic virgin of Alexandria. At 18, she debated the Faith with 50 pagan philosophers—and converted them! The emperor Maximus martyred all of them, and ordered Catherine to be imprisoned and scourged. In prison Catherine converted the emperor's wife and 200 of his soldiers. The enraged Maximus then ordered Catherine to be executed on a spiked wheel. It shattered at her touch, and he beheaded Catherine in 305 AD. Devotion to Saint Catherine spread during the Crusades, and students, teachers, librarians, and lawyers especially asked for her patronage.

Saint Catherine of Alexandria, pray for us!

Saint Dymphna

Patroness of Those who suffer Emotional and Mental Illness

Feast Day: May 15

Saint Dymphna's mother died when she was only 14. When her father could find no one else suitable in his eyes to marry, he became mentally ill and made advances on his beautiful daughter. Saint Dymphna fled to Belgium, where her father found her and martyred her in 620 AD. Many people have been healed miraculously at her shrine, built on the spot where she was buried in Gheel, Belgium.

Saint Dymphna, pray for us!

Writers and Warriors

Saint Alice

Patroness of Cheerful Suffering

Feast Day: June 15

Saint Alice was born in Belgium in the early 13th century. At an early age she entered the convent, and the sisters loved her especially for her humility. Shortly thereafter, Alice was struck with leprosy, a dread disease which caused her to spend the rest of her life in isolation. Even so, her cheerful spirit brought great strength to her sisters. Her greatest joy was to receive our Lord in the Holy Eucharist. Alice offered her suffering for all, especially the souls in purgatory, and God rewarded her with His unending love and victory. ***Saint Alice, pray for us!***

Saint Gertrude

Patroness of Nuns

Feast Day: November 16

At the age of 5, Saint Gertrude was taken into a convent by the Benedictine Nuns at Helfta, Germany. She enjoyed studying, and God granted her the graces of various mystical experiences, including a vision of Jesus, who invited her to rest her head on His breast to hear the beating of His heart. Saint Gertrude kept a journal of her many visions in her *Book of Extraordinary Grace* and wrote many prayers as well. Her devotion to the Sacred Heart of Jesus is expressed beautifully in her many writings. Saint Gertrude died in 1301.
Saint Gertrude, pray for us!

Saint Catherine of Siena

Patroness of Purity

Feast Day: April 29

Catherine of Siena, who was born in 1347, loved to pray and even had visions of angels. At the age of 15, Catherine entered the Third Order of Saint Dominic. She loved to pray quietly alone with God, and then serve others with love and joy. Catherine traveled through Italy, bringing people back to obedience to the Pope, and winning hardened souls to God. Saint Catherine—mystic, stigmatist, visionary, miracle worker, counselor, and writer—died at the age of 33. In 1970, Pope Paul VI declared Saint Catherine of Siena a Doctor of the Church.
Saint Catherine of Siena, pray for us!

Saint Joan of Arc

Patroness of Servicewomen

Feast Day: May 30

Joan of Arc was born in France in 1412. As a shepherdess, she heard some of the saints speak personally to her, telling her to help King Charles VII of France conquer his enemies. Joan was only 17 when she helped end the siege of Orleans. After winning many battles, she was kidnapped by her enemies and tricked into saying things that made her sound like a heretic. Joan was only 19 when she was burned at the stake, but her faith in God was eventually recognized and in 1920 she was canonized as Saint Joan of Arc.
Saint Joan of Arc, pray for us!

Wives and Reformers

Saint Rita

Patroness of Impossible or Lost Causes

Feast Day: May 22

Saint Rita was born in Italy in 1381. Rita wanted to devote her life to God and become a nun, but her parents arranged for her to marry a man who later proved to be neglectful, abusive and unfaithful. After 18 unhappy years of marriage, Saint Rita's husband was killed, and Rita entered a convent. One day as she knelt in prayer, her forehead was miraculously pierced by a thorn from the Crown of Thorns. Saint Rita died 15 years later and was canonized in 1900.

Saint Rita, pray for us.

Saint Teresa of Avila

Patroness of those suffering with headaches

Feast Day: October 15

Saint Teresa was born in Avila, Spain, in 1515. At age 18, she entered the Carmelite monastery. During this time Teresa suffered from painful headaches. She was cured through Saint Joseph's intercession, and she began to see suffering in the light of the Cross. Conditions at the convent motivated Teresa to establish the Reform of the Discalced Carmelites. She established 32 monasteries and left behind a collection of writings which have made a significant contribution to learning in the Church. Saint Teresa was the first woman to be named a Doctor of the Church in 1970.

Saint Teresa of Avila, pray for us.

Saint Rose of Lima

Patroness of Florists

Feast Day: August 23

Rose's birth name in her native Peru was Isabel, but her parents found her to be so lovely that they called her 'Rose.' Rose's love for Jesus only increased her outer beauty, as His intimate presence in her life shone out in her life of service to others, especially the poor. In 1606, Rose joined the Dominican Third Order. Her life was filled with physical, emotional, and spiritual suffering, yet God increased His love in her heart as she offered herself to Him. Rose died at the age of 31.

Saint Rose of Lima, pray for us.

Founders and Mystics

Saint Louise de Marillac

Patroness of Social Workers

Feast Day: March 15

Louise de Marillac was born in France in 1591; by the age of 15 she lost her parents. Louise married shortly thereafter, but her husband died four years later, and she came under the direction of Saint Vincent de Paul. He sent her on missions to the poor and sick, and soon other young women joined their ministry. With Saint Vincent, Louise founded the Daughters of Charity in 1642. The small community sought to aid the numerous neglected children on the streets, establishing hospitals and orphanages. By the time of her death in 1660, Saint Louise de Marillac had founded over 40 houses in France. Her incorrupt body today lies in the chapel of the Daughters of Charity in Paris.

Saint Louise de Marillac, pray for us!

Saint Margaret Mary

Patroness of Devotion to the Sacred Heart

Feast Day: October 17

Born in 1647, Margaret Mary Alacoque was crippled by a disease at age 8. After promising to give her life to Jesus, she was cured by the Blessed Virgin Mary. At 23, she entered the Visitation Order. Jesus appeared to Sister Margaret Mary, showing her four visions of His Sacred Heart. The flames coming forth from Jesus' Heart remind us of His burning love for us and His desire that we love Him in return. Jesus revealed to Margaret Mary that she was His chosen instrument to spread devotion to His Sacred Heart, instructed her in the First Friday devotions and the Holy Hour, and asked that a feast to His Sacred Heart be established. Saint Margaret Mary died in 1690, and was canonized in 1920. **Saint Margaret Mary, pray for us!**

Saint Kateri Tekakwitha

Lily of the Mohawks, Co-Patroness of Environment and Ecology

Feast Day: July 14

Tekakwitha—*She who bumps into things*—was born to a Mohawk warrior father and a Christian Algonquin mother near Auriesville, New York in 1656. Her parents died in a smallpox epidemic that left Tekakwitha with weakened eyesight and her face scarred for life. She told the Jesuit "Blackrobes" that she wanted to be a Christian, and on Easter Sunday, 1676, Kateri (Catherine) Tekakwitha was baptized. Kateri, who greatly loved Our Lord and His Mother Mary, escaped from her disapproving family by journeying many miles to Sault Sainte Marie, Canada. Kateri kindly cared for children, the sick, and the elderly. After a long bout with illness, she died on April 17, 1680. Pope John Paul II beatified Kateri, and on February 18, 2012, Pope Benedict XVI canonized Kateri Tekakwitha, the first Native American to be declared a Saint!

Saint Kateri Tekakwitha, pray for us!

Teachers and Visionaries

Saint Elizabeth Ann Seton

Patroness of Converts
Feast Day: January 4

Elizabeth Seton was born in 1774. She married William Seton, but he left her a young widow with their five children. Elizabeth became a Catholic and founded the Sisters of Charity, beginning the American parochial school system. Mother Seton died in 1821, and became the first native-born American to be canonized!

Saint Elizabeth Ann Seton, pray for us!

Saint Bernadette Soubirous

Patroness of the Sick
Feast Day: April 16

Bernadette Soubirous was born in Lourdes on January 7, 1844. In 1858, the Virgin Mary appeared to her in a cave near the Gave River. At Mary's request, Bernadette dug at a spot nearby, from which a spring emerged with healing waters. Our Lady also requested that a church be built at the site. In 1866, Bernadette joined the Sisters of Notre Dame, and died there in 1879. Pope Pius XI canonized Saint Bernadette in 1933.

Saint Bernadette, pray for us!

Saint Therese of Lisieux

Patroness of the Missions
Feast Day: October 1

Therese Martin was born in France in 1873. Her beloved mother died when Therese was still young, and she joined the Carmelite Order. Loving and trusting in God as a child was her "little way." Therese died at the age of 24, whispering, "My God, I love You!" Saint Therese was named a Doctor of the Church by Pope John Paul II.

Saint Therese of Lisieux, pray for us!

Saint Catherine Labouré

Patroness of Devotion to the Miraculous Medal
Feast Day: November 25

Catherine Labouré was born in 1806, and entered the Daughters of Charity in Paris at age 24. One night Mother Mary appeared to Catherine, asking her to have a medal struck with the words, "O Mary, conceived without sin, pray for us who have recourse to thee." Our Lady told Catherine that wearers of the medal would receive great graces. Saint Catherine Labouré died on December 31, 1876, a true daughter of Jesus and Mary to the very end.

Saint Catherine Labouré, pray for us!

Saint Frances Cabrini

Patroness of Immigrants
Feast Day: November 13

Frances Xavier Cabrini was born in Italy in 1850. She founded the Missionary Sisters of the Sacred Heart to care for poor children in schools and hospitals. Mother Cabrini came to the United States and founded schools, hospitals, and orphanages to help the Italian immigrants. Mother Frances Xavier Cabrini died in 1917, and in 1946, became the first American citizen to be canonized!

Saint Frances Cabrini, pray for us!